Simple Gluten Free, Dairy Free, Soy Free, and Nightshade Free Holiday Recipes

Familiar Menu Ideas with recipes your family will know and love.

By Paula C. Henderson

Cover designed by Paula C. Henderson

ISBN: 9781706207757

Paula C. Henderson
Visit my website at www.Monumental-Ladies.us

Printed in the United States of America

First Printing: November 2019

Amazon Authors Page:
www.amazon.com/author/paulachenderson

Table of Contents

It's the holidays! As long as the food is gluten free, dairy free, soy free and nightshade free I am including it. Since this is a holiday menu we are not going to concern ourselves with making sure it is 100% healthy. So you will find carbonated beverages like cola and soda's listed because they do, in fact, qualify.

Some general guidelines:

The following are gluten and dairy free:
- All meat
- All seafood
- All vegetables
- All fruits
- All oil
- All vinegar, with the exception of malt vinegar

While *edamame (soybeans) are gluten and dairy free, they are not soy free. Vegetable Oil is soybean oil so choose another oil and be sure to glance at the ingredients. *Goji berries are gluten free, dairy free, and soy free but they are one of the few fruits that are a nightshade.

A list of soy products to avoid:

Soybean oil, tofu, edamame beans, soy milk, soy nuts, soy sauce, tempeh, and miso. Many plant based meat alternatives contain soy.

A list of nightshades to avoid:
- Tomatoes
- White and red potatoes (not sweet potatoes or yams)
- Eggplant

- All peppers (not black pepper and not onions)

- All of the byproducts from these foods like crushed red pepper, hot sauce, catsup and paprika.

Remember that you can always place condiments and rolls on the table for your guests who can eat hot sauce, catsup and other gluten, dairy, soy and nightshade food products.

Bread

There are many, many choices to choose from when looking for a gluten free bread. If you are avoiding nightshades be sure to glance at the ingredients list so you can be sure to avoid potato starch. Many of us, including me, can have the occasional potato starch in gluten free bread so long as I am otherwise very strictly following a nightshade free diet.

To find all of the gluten free breads your grocer has to offer check the bread aisle, the freezer section usually included around the frozen breakfast foods, and I have also found gluten free breads in the bakery. Even if you do not find rolls that would suit your holiday dinner, you can get the sandwich bread to make bread crumbs, croutons, dressing and stuffing or Christmas morning French toast.

BEVERAGES

- Water
- Tea
- Lemonade
- Sparkling Water
- Coffee
- Carbonated Beverages like cola and soda.
- Juice
- Kool-aid

Adult Beverages:

- Champagne
- Rum (plain unflavored rum only)
- Tequila
- Wine

Vodka is generally made from potatoes, a nightshade. Beer and whiskey are a gluten. Having said that there are many brands who have come out with gluten free beer and whiskey so feel free to check your local stores and be sure to read the label.

Remember that you can use coconut milk, bitters, and triple sec which are all gluten free, dairy free, soy free and nightshade free to make drinks.

- 1.5 cups gold tequila
- ¾ cup triple sec
- ¾ cup fresh lime juice
- 4 tablespoons sugar
- 8 cups crushed ice
- 2 tablespoons kosher salt
- 6 lime wedges

Mix the tequila, triple sec, lime juice, and the sugar I a large pitcher.
Stir to dissolve the sugar.
Add crushed ice.
In a small bowl mix the salt and a couple teaspoons of sugar.
Using a lime wedge, moisten each glass rim and then dip the glass upside down in the salt and sugar mixture.
Add the margarita mix to the glass, garnish with a lime wedge.

Orange juice and champagne!
Generally you pour 2 ounces of orange juice into the flute glass and then fill the remaining of the glass with champagne.

- 1/5 cups ice
- 1.2 cup diced pineapple, frozen
- 2 ounces pineapple juice
- 2 ounces canned coconut cream fat (allow the can to refrigerate overnight and then remove the cream (don't shake the can)
- 1/5 ounces white rum
- 1 ounce dark rum

Place the ice, frozen pineapple, juice, coconut cream and both rums into the blender. Blend well.

APPETIZERS

Menu ideas:

- A vegetable tray with dip
- chips and choice of dips
- olives
- mixed nuts
- deviled eggs
- stuffed mushrooms
- cocktail franks

Oh, and bacon wrapped anything! Remember, the appetizers can always overflow to the dinner table.

Bacon Wrapped Dates

- 30-40 pitted dates
- 2 pounds bacon (thin standard, not thick cut)

Preheat oven to 425.

Cut the bacon in half.
Wrap each date with a piece of bacon and secure with a toothpick.
Place on a baking sheet (do not overcrowd. Use two baking sheets if necessary).
Bake about 15-20 minutes total.
Turn over halfway through baking. Best served warm.

Chips:

- White or Yellow Corn tortilla chips
- Rice crackers
- Pork Rinds (regular: not spicy)

Cocktail Franks

- 1 pound gluten free cocktail franks. Hillshire Farm's is gluten free.
- 1 eight ounce jar of grape jelly or cranberry sauce
- 1 8 ounce jar of prepared yellow mustard

In a saucepan, heat the jelly and mustard until well combined.
Stir in cocktail wieners.
You could also use a crockpot.
I suggest combining the jelly and mustard prior to adding to the crockpot.
Serve with toothpicks!

Deviled Eggs

- 6 hard-boiled eggs
- ¼ cup mayo
- 1 teaspoon white vinegar
- 1 teaspoon yellow mustard
- 1/8 teaspoon salt
- Black pepper to taste

If you like to add a bit of paprika to the top, try cumin instead.

Place eggs in water, covered.
Then place on stove and bring to a boil, uncovered.
When the eggs come to a full boil, remove from heat and cover immediately.
Allow eggs to sit in water, covered for 15 minutes.

Peel eggs, slice in half, and separate egg yolk from egg white.

Combine egg yolks with mayo, mustard, salt, pepper, and vinegar.
Stuff in the egg whites.
Refrigerate until time to serve.
I like to top mine with thinly sliced green onions.

Gluten Free Chex Party Mix:

Chex Christmas Snack Mix can easily be prepared gluten free, dairy free, soy free and nightshade free:

- 9 cups of Gluten Free Rice Chex and Corn Chex
- 1 cup mixed nuts
- 6 tablespoons healthy oil or dairy free butter
- 2 tablespoons Lea & Perrins Worcestershire Sauce (one of the few brands that are gluten free)
- ¾ teaspoon garlic powder
- ½ teaspoon onion powder

Preheat oven to 250 degrees
Melt butter or heat oil in roasting pan.
Stir in all ingredients, coating well.
Spread evenly and bake one full hour.
Be sure to stir every 15 minutes.

Pickles and Olives

Pickles and olives are fine with just a few exceptions. Avoid those described as spicy. Check the ingredients list just to be sure the ingredient *spices* is not listed. The generic term *spices* generally includes a nightshade. Also avoid olives that have a pimento or remove the pimento.

Vegetable Tray:

Gluten free, dairy free, soy free, nightshade free vegetable list for your relish tray:

- Broccoli
- Carrots
- Cauliflower
- Celery
- Cucumbers
- Endive
- Green onions (scallions)
- Jicama
- Olives (no pimento: it's a nightshade)
- Pearl Onions
- Pickles (non-spicy. Check the ingredients list to be sure there are no nightshades)
- Radishes
- Sugar Snap Peas

Dips:

Crab Dip

- 2 cups lump crab meat
- 1 teaspoon mustard
- 2 tablespoons minced red onion
- 1 cup mayo
- 1.5 teaspoons lemon juice
- ½ teaspoon garlic powder
- ½ teaspoon black pepper (double to add heat)
- ½ teaspoon salt
- Optional: ½ cup pureed canned artichokes

Combine all of the ingredients well.

Bake in a preheated 350 degree oven for about 15 minutes. Should be bubbly.

Hit the top just for a moment to get a nice browning on the top if needed.

If you have a dairy free substitute for parmesans cheese that is certainly a nice topping or gluten free breadcrumbs you make yourself using gluten free sandwich bread.

Seasoned Breadcrumbs

Coat each slice of bread with olive oil, garlic powder, salt and pepper. Bake in a 400 degree preheated oven on a baking sheet until golden brown. Allow to cool. Place in a ziploc baggie or your food processor and make your breadcrumbs.

Deviled Crab Dip

- ½ pound crabmeat
- 3 tablespoons mayo
- 1 tablespoon mustard
- ½ teaspoon lemon juice
- ½ teaspoon pepper
- ¼ teaspoon gluten free Worcestershire Sauce

Mix all together and chill before serving.

Guacamole

- 2 avocados (ripe)
- 2 tablespoons red onion
- 2 tablespoons chopped fresh cilantro
- ½ teaspoon salt

Combine all ingredients right before serving.

Hummus

- 1 can chick peas (garbanzo beans), 19oz, drained
- 5 tablespoons water
- 4 tablespoons lemon juice
- 2 tablespoons tahini (try sesame oil if you do not have tahini)
- ½ teaspoon salt (more to taste)
- ½ teaspoon lemon pepper
- 1-2 clove garlic

- 2-4 tablespoons olive oil (more if needed)

In a blender, add the beans, water, lemon juice, tahini or sesame oil, salt and pepper.
Blend until smooth.
Add more oil to the right consistency.
Once smooth and creamy, add the garlic and pulse a couple times to combine.
Refrigerate until time to serve.

Refried Bean Dip

- 1 can refried beans (15ounce)
- ¼ cup minced onion
- 2 tablespoons minced garlic
- ½ teaspoon salt
- 1/8 teaspoon cumin
- ½ teaspoon black pepper
- 1 teaspoon lime juice

Combine all ingredients well.
Add a tablespoon of water if too thick.
Refrigerate until time to serve. Or prepare and heat and serve immediately.
This is usually served warm but can be served cold.

Roasted Garlic White Bean Dip

- 1 can of northern beans (15oz), rinsed and drained
- 4 tablespoons olive oil
- ½ teaspoon salt
- ½ teaspoon pepper (or to taste)
- 2-3 teaspoons minced garlic (more to taste)
- 2 teaspoons cumin
- 1/3 cup pureed (drained) canned artichokes
- 4 tablespoons minced onion (more to taste)

Combine the beans, oil, salt and pepper, cumin, artichokes in a food processor or blender.
Blend until smooth and creamy.
Add garlic and onion. Pulse a few times to blend well.
Taste and adjust salt and garlic.
Add lemon juice if you feel it needs a zing.
Add more black pepper for more heat.

Refrigerate for at least one hour.

Spinach-Artichoke Dip

Fresh or frozen spinach will work. If you are using frozen spinach go straight to the saucepan from the freezer.

- 1 pound bag of frozen spinach or 3 pounds fresh
- One 15oz can artichokes (with the liquid)
- 1 tablespoon oil or dairy free butter
- 1 tablespoon corn starch
- 2 garlic cloves, smash, minced
- 1 teaspoon garlic powder
- 1 teaspoon onion powder
- 1 tablespoon apple cider vinegar
- ½ cup water
- Salt and pepper to taste

Puree the artichokes with the liquid.

Heat the butter or oil in a saucepan, add the corn starch and stir to make a roux. Add the water and the garlic, salt and pepper. Continue to stir. Should thicken rather quickly.

Add the pureed artichokes and the spinach. Combine well.

Add the remaining ingredients. Taste and adjust salt and pepper.

Allow this to simmer med/low to allow for the liquid to cook down. About 15-20 minutes.

Optional: transfer to a baking dish, top with Seasoned Breadcrumbs (recipe under Crab Dip).

Bake in preheated 400 degree oven for about 5-10 minutes just until the breadcrumbs have browned.

Fruit Plate

- Apple slices
- Cantaloupe
- Dried fruit and nuts
- Grapes
- Kiwi slices
- Melon
- Pear slices
- Pineapple
- Strawberries
- Sweet cherries
- Watermelon

You can, of course, use an apple slicer for quarters. For a more elegant look try thinly slicing the quartered sections.

Mixed Nuts

All nuts and seeds are gluten free, dairy free, and nightshade free. **Avoid soy nuts.** You can make your own or buy mixed nuts. Just stay away from seasoned or spicy. Salted is okay.

Popcorn

Popcorn is a great item to set out with mixed nuts, chips and dip and a vegetable tray.

Sugar Coated Pecans

- 1 pound pecan halves
- 1 cup sugar
- 1 egg white, beaten
- 1 tablespoon water
- ¾ teaspoon salt
- ½ teaspoon cinnamon

Preheat your oven to 250 degrees.

Grease a baking sheet.

Mix the egg white and water in a bowl.

In a separate bowl, mix the cinnamon, sugar and salt.

Coat the pecan halves in the egg white first, then the sugar mix and layout onto the baking sheet.

Bake for 1 full hour. Be sure to stir the pecans around on the baking sheet every 15 minutes while baking.

Stuffed Mushrooms

- 2 pounds white button mushrooms with the stems removed but reserved.
- 1/2 cup of the Bread Stuffing (recipe in side dishes)
- Ground pork (from the meat department in the Styrofoam tray.
- 1 teaspoon ground sage
- ½ teaspoon salt
- ½ teaspoon pepper

Preheat oven to 325.

Clean and remove the stems of the mushrooms.

Rub each mushroom cap with oil and place on a baking sheet.

Brown the ground pork, adding the chopped up mushroom stems.

Salt the pork as soon as you put it into the skillet before it starts to brown.

Add the prepared Bread Stuffing or Cornbread Dressing from the Side Dish recipes. Combine well and heat through.

Stuff each mushroom with the dressing/sausage mixture.

Bake about 35-40 minutes until golden brown and mushrooms are tender.

MAIN COURSE

MEAT

All meats, in and of themselves are gluten free, dairy free, soy free and nightshade free. Just be sure to buy your meat or seafood in the meat and seafood department, not frozen foods. Avoid seasoned meats. Buy whole turkey, whole chicken or hen, ham or roast. Many times pre-seasoned meats contain gluten and/or nightshades. Prepare your meat or seafood however you normally do. Just avoid using flour (try cornstarch or rice flour instead). Avoid seasoning packets as they too generally contain nightshades or gluten and sometimes soy.

When seasoning for yourself, avoid the following seasonings that are nightshades: crushed red pepper, cayenne, All Seasoning, seasoning packets, and paprika. Use oil instead of butter. Avocado Oil is actually a nice replacement for melted butter as far as flavor goes. Here are the most common meats prepared during the holidays, but all meats and all seafood's (that being the only ingredient) are all gluten free, dairy free, soy free and nightshade free.

Chicken and Turkey

- Turkey
- Roasted Duck
- Game Hens

I have found a standard guide to baking whole turkey, hens or chickens:

Clean out the cavity
Place in a baking dish breast up
Rub the bird with oil and then salt and pepper. I prefer to stop there but you can certainly add other seasonings like sage, lemon pepper, rosemary, thyme.
Cover loosely with foil when you first place in the oven.
Bake in a pre-heated 375 degree oven

Bake 20 minutes per pound plus 15. The last 15 minutes bake without the foil.

So let's say you are baking a 5 pound bird. You would bake for (20 minutes x 5 pounds = 100 minutes, or one hour and forty minutes. Remove the foil and continue to bake 15 minutes. You should otherwise follow the directions on the packaging.

Ham

Tips for baking your very best whole ham:

Most holiday hams will weigh about 8 pounds.

Be sure to score the ham. Use a paring knife and make criss-cross knife cuts like we often see in pictures.

Place on your baking sheet. Use a piece of foil sprayed with non-stick cooking spray over the baking sheet to prevent sticking and make clean up a bit easier.

Preheat your oven to 300 degrees.

Brown Sugar Glaze

Combine in a glass bowl:

- ½ cup brown sugar
- 1 tablespoon lime juice
- 1/8 teaspoon ground cloves
- ½ teaspoon cinnamon
- 1/2 teaspoon ground ginger
- ½ teaspoon black pepper
- ½ teaspoon salt

Spread evenly over the scored ham.

Bake 15 minutes per pound.

Horseradish, often used for beef, is fine to eat. It is gluten free, dairy free, soy free and nightshade free. If you are going to buy horseradish in a jar be sure to check the label and some do add soybean oil.

Prime Rib

- 5-7 pounds prime rib
- ¼ cup oil
- ¼ cup prepared horseradish
- 1 teaspoon Salt
- 1 tablespoon coarse black pepper

Preheat oven to 500 degrees.

Combine oil, salt, horseradish and black pepper in a bowl.
Rub evenly over the prime rib (except the bottom that will be against the pan).

Bake on a rack in a roasting pan for 40 minutes (about 5 minutes per pound).

When the 40 minutes is up leave the meat in the oven but turn off the oven.

Allow the meat to sit inside for another 1.5 hours. Do not open the oven door.

Horseradish sauce:

- 1 cup mayo
- 1 tablespoon horseradish
- Salt and pepper to taste

Combine well.

Pork Tenderloin with Onion Jam

Preheat oven to 425 degrees.

Prepare the onion jam: heat the oil in a skillet and add the onion.
Cooking until the onion is soft and beginning to brown.
Remove onion and add the bacon, cut into bite size pieces.
Fry bacon, remove and reserve bacon fat.
Combine the onions and bacon.
In a saucepan, combine the bacon, onions, brown sugar and broth.
Cook over medium/low heat and allow liquid to cook down: about half hour. Once this has reduced, add the vinegar.

Pat the tenderloin dry with paper towels and sprinkle well with salt and pepper.

Heat the bacon fat that was left in the skillet.
Brown the tenderloin on all sides with a quick sear.
Bake the seared pork tenderloin in the preheated 425 oven for about 20 minutes.
Add the onion and bacon back to the skillet you just removed the tenderloin from.
Cook on low while pork tenderloin is baking.
Stir the onions often.

Onion Jam

- 1 large yellow onion
- 2 tablespoons oil
- 1/3 cup brown sugar
- ¼ cup beef broth
- 1 tablespoons apple cider vinegar
- Bacon (optional)

Rack of Lamb

- 1 Lamb Rack
- ¼ cup cooking oil
- 3 garlic cloves, minced
- 2 rosemary sprigs
- 4 thyme sprigs
- Salt and Black pepper

Scrape rib bones with a paring knife to expose the bones.

Cut the racks into four rib sections.

Combine the oil, garlic, salt and pepper. Rub onto the meat coating it well.

Lay the rosemary sprigs and thyme sprigs in the pan. Cover and marinate overnight.

Next day:

Preheat oven to 400 degrees.

Using a spatula scrape any loose pieces of garlic off the meat to the bottom of the pan. Salt lightly once more.

In a hot oiled skillet, sear the fat side of the lamb about 5 minutes, just until golden brown.

Transfer to the oven and bake about 18-25 minutes.

It's very important to allow the lamb to rest at least 10 minutes before slicing or serving.

Lobster Tails

- 4 lobster tails
- 1 gallon water
- 4 bay leaves
- 1 bunch fresh parsley
- 16 ounces melted dairy free butter or Avocado Oil

Boil **salted** water, bay leaves and parsley in a large stock pot.

Once the water is at a full boil add the lobster tails.

Cover, and boil about 10 minutes. Remove and set aside.

The meat should look white and meaty, no longer translucent.

If this is your first time, take a good look at how the meat looks prior to boiling.

Salmon

- 2 pounds salmon. (for the holidays it's quite impressive to serve the whole salmon from the seafood department on a nice serving platter, rather than the individual filets but either will work fine.)
- 2 tablespoons oil
- ¼ cup brown sugar
- ¼ cup coconut aminos (this is an alternative to soy sauce. If you cannot find this in your store it is available online but most stores have it available now)
- 3 garlic cloves, minced
- Juice of one lemon
- ½ teaspoon black pepper

Preheat oven to 350.

Line a baking sheet with foil, spray with non-stick cooking spray.
Lay the salmon on the baking sheet and salt and pepper.

Before this next part you will want to lift all four sides of the foil up to make sort of a bowl.

In a small bowl, whisk together the oil, sugar, coconut aminos, garlic, and the juice of one lemon.
Pour over the salmon and then tightly seal the foil around the salmon.

Bake in your preheated 350 oven for 20-25 minutes.
Open the foil, baste the salmon and then return to the oven set on broil for just 3-5 minutes to lightly brown the top.

Serve!

SIDE DISHES

All vegetables and all fruits are gluten free and dairy free.

....not all vegetables are nightshade free and soy free.

Soy vegetables to avoid:

Edamame beans (soybeans)

Nightshade Vegetables to Avoid:

- Bell pepper
- Catsup/ketchup (a byproduct)
- Cayenne pepper (byproduct)
- Chili and Taco Seasoning packets (byproduct)
- Chili powder (byproduct)
- Chinese five spice (byproduct)
- Crushed red pepper (byproduct)
- Eggplant
- Hot peppers
- Hot sauce (byproduct)
- Paprika (byproduct)
- Pepperoncini
- Pimento
- Red potatoes
- Steak Seasoning (byproduct)
- Tomatillos
- Tomatoes
- White potatoes (for example russet and Idaho)

*FAQ about nightshades: The following are **NOT** nightshades and are okay to eat:*

Black Pepper
Cumin
Onions
Sweet Potatoes, Yams and White Sweet Potatoes

Acorn Squash

- 4 Acorn Squash
- 4 tablespoons melted dairy free butter
- 4 tablespoons pure maple syrup
- Olive oil
- Salt and pepper

Preheat oven to 350

Cut the squash in half through the stem. Remove the seeds.
Place the squash, cut side up on a baking sheet. Salt and pepper each squash.
Spread butter and the pure maple syrup on each squash.
Bake about 45-50 minutes until tender.

Asparagus

Oven roasted asparagus

- One pound fresh asparagus
- ¼ cup oil
- 1 teaspoon salt
- 1 teaspoon lemon pepper

Toss asparagus with oil, salt and pepper.
Spread onto a baking sheet.
Bake in a 425 degree oven about 15 minutes until tender and golden brown. It's important to not crowd the asparagus. Use two baking sheets if you need to.

Brussels Sprouts

I have used fresh and frozen brussels sprouts and they both work just fine.
1 pound whole brussels sprouts (fresh or frozen). Cut into halves.

Toss the brussels sprouts with oil, salt and pepper. Straight out of the freezer if using frozen, cut in half and toss.

Preheat oven to 400 degrees. Spread brussels sprouts onto a baking sheet. Do not overcrowd. Us two baking sheets if necessary.

Bake until golden brown and tender.
Spritz with balsamic vinegar before serving.
If you aren't sure about the vinegar (lemon juice is a find substitute), just spritz one or two, try it and then decide.

Butternut Squash

- 2 medium size butternut squash
- 8 tablespoons dairy free butter or cooking oil
- ¼ cup brown sugar
- 1.5 teaspoons salt
- ½ teaspoon black pepper

Preheat oven to 400

Remove both ends of the squash and discard.
Peel, cut lengthwise and remove the seeds.
Then cut into bite size pieces.
Toss squash in a bowl with melted butter or oil, sugar, salt and pepper.
Spread onto a baking sheet.

Bake about 55 minutes, turning halfway through baking.

Cauliflower Medley

- 1 head of fresh cauliflower, chopped to small bite size pieces
- 2 large carrots, peeled and chopped
- 2 stalks of celery, chopped
- 1 package baby bella mushrooms
- 1 small onion, chopped
- 4 tablespoons cooking oil
- 2 tablespoons rosemary
- 1 teaspoons ground sage
- 1 teaspoon salt
- 1 teaspoon black pepper
- ½ cup chicken broth

Add oil to a skillet and sauté the onion, carrot, and celery until just soft.

Add the cauliflower and the mushrooms, and all of the seasonings to the skillet.

Add broth and allow to simmer until the broth has cooked down. Stir often.

Carrots

- 16 ounce bag carrots (your choice of whole, baby, or pre-cut sticks)
- 2 tablespoon dairy free butter or oil. Avocado oil works nice in this dish
- 1 cup chicken broth or water
- Salt to taste (start with ½ teaspoon)
- ½ teaspoon black or white pepper

Using a saucepan, combine the carrots, butter or oil, sugar and the water. Stir to blend well.

Bring to a boil.

Reduce heat to med/low leaving uncovered and allow to simmer about 20 minutes or until the carrots are tender.

The liquid should cook down so stay near to avoid burning. Add small amounts of water if needed while cooking.

That's it! Serve hot. When you place the carrots in a serving dish, take the time to have all of the carrots the same direction for a nice presentation.

Roasted Carrots

- 1 pound raw carrots (cut the larger carrots lengthwise)
- 4 tablespoons oil
- 1.5 teaspoons salt
- ½ teaspoon black pepper
- 2 tablespoons minced parsley

Preheat oven to 400 degrees.

Cut each carrot in half with a diagonal cut, two cuts on longer carrots. Each piece should be about 2 inches long.

Toss carrots in a bowl with oil, salt and pepper.

Spread the carrots onto a baking sheet. Make sure not to crowd. Use two baking sheets if necessary.

Bake about 20 minutes or until tender and starting to brown.

Toss the carrots with parsley before serving.

Corny Cornbread

- 2 cups yellow cornmeal
- 1 tablespoon sugar
- 1 teaspoon salt
- 2 teaspoons baking powder
- ½ teaspoon baking soda
- 1 cup chicken broth
- 2 whole eggs
- 1 egg yolk
- One 15 ounce can creamed corn
- 2 tablespoons oil

Preheat oven to 425

Place the cast iron skillet in the oven to heat.

Combine cornmeal, salt, sugar, baking powder, baking soda.

In a second bowl, combine broth, eggs and yolk, creamed corn.
Then add the dry ingredients to the wet ingredients.
Should be about the consistency of pancake batter.
If the batter is too thick add a bit more broth.

Remove the hot skillet, add oil and spread though-out the skillet.
Pour the batter into the skillet.
Bake about 20 minutes.

Cranberry Sauce

Canned cranberry sauce is gluten free, dairy free, soy free and nightshade free.

You can also make your fresh cranberry sauce:

- 12 ounce bag fresh cranberries (washed)
- 1 cup sugar
- 1 tablespoon orange zest
- 1 tablespoon fresh squeezed orange juice
- 2 tablespoons water

Place cranberries in a saucepan.
Add one cup sugar to saucepan along with zest, juice and water.
Cook over low heat stirring often about 10 minutes or until the cranberries are soft and bursted.

Creamed Corn

- 6 slices bacon
- 8 ears of corn
- Salt and pepper

Cook the bacon nice and crispy. Set aside.

Shave the kernels off the cob (this method is noticeably better than using canned or frozen corn).

Keep as much of the liquid that releases while shaving off the kernels. Transfer corn and all of the liquid released to the skillet with the bacon fat, add salt and pepper. If it appears you have less than 1 cup of liquid, make up the difference using water.

Simmer the corn for about 45 minutes and stir often. Corn should be tender. Toss with crumbled bacon at the time of serving.

Cucumber Onion Salad

- 2 cucumbers, peeled and sliced
- 1 red onion, sliced on the vein (cut the onion in half. Lay each half on the onions flat side. Slice along the green vein for half-moon shaped pieces.
- 1 tablespoon white wine vinegar
- 1 teaspoon sugar
- 1 tablespoon water
- Salt and Pepper

Combine all in a glass dish. Cover tightly and keep chilled until time to serve.

Tip: combine the vinegar, water, sugar, salt and pepper in a jar first so you can shake it and it combines well. The toss with the cucumber and onions.

Dressing and Stuffing

- Gluten free skillet of cornbread: using gluten free cornmeal, make a 9 inch skillet of cornbread. Or two if doubling to a large casserole dish.
- 2 cups thinly sliced celery
- 1 cup finely chopped onion
- 2 tablespoons sage
- 1 teaspoon thyme
- 5-10 cups rich chicken broth
- 1 teaspoon salt
- 1 teaspoon black pepper
- 4 tablespoons cooking oil or melted dairy free butter alternative

Skillet of Cornbread:

- 2 cups self-rising gluten free cornmeal
- 2 eggs
- 6 tablespoons oil or melted dairy free butter (actually melted coconut oil works well here)
- 1 teaspoon white sugar
- 1 teaspoon salt
- 1-2 cups chicken broth

Preheat oven to 425.

Place the oil in a 9 inch cast iron skillet and heat until very hot but not smoking.

While this heats:

In a large bowl whisk eggs. Add 1 cup of broth, sugar, salt and the cornmeal. Stir well.
Add more broth if needed for the consistency of a pancake batter.

Grab the skillet out of the oven and carefully add the hot oil to the batter. Combine. While the skillet is still quite hot pour the batter into the hot skillet.
Bake about 20 minutes or so until a toothpick comes out clean.

Transfer the baked cornbread into a large bowl, allowing it to break apart.
Add the onions, celery, sage, thyme, salt and pepper.
Add broth one cup at a time. Combining well. Should be the consistency of mashed potatoes.
Spread evenly into a greased casserole dish (13x9)

Bake in a preheated 350 degree oven, uncovered, for about an hour or until golden brown on top and the edges should be crispy.

- o   2 loaves Gluten free sliced bread
- o   2 small onions, chopped
- o   4 stalks of celery, chopped
- 8 tablespoons cooking oil
- 2 garlic cloves, minced
- 1 teaspoon ground sage
- 1 teaspoon thyme
- ½ teaspoon rosemary
- 1 teaspoon salt
- ½ teaspoon black pepper
- 2 cups chicken broth

Preheat your oven to 350.

Oil a large baking dish.

In a skillet, on the stove: sauté onion and celery until soft. Stir in garlic, sage, thyme and rosemary along with salt and pepper.
Cook about one full minute.

Place bread in a large bowl and add vegetables from the skillet as well as the broth. Combine well.

Bake in your preheated oven (covered with foil) about 45 minutes.
Remove foil and continue to bake another 15 minutes.

Fried Apples

This is a great side dish, or makes a very tasty dessert when served with whipped cream. Or serve over French Toast for brunch or breakfast.

- ½ cup dairy free butter
- 6 medium unpeeled tart apples
- ¾ cup brown sugar
- ¾ teaspoon cinnamon

Melt butter in a skillet.

Add apples and half of the sugar. Stir to coat well.

Cover and cook over low heat for about 20 minutes or until apples are tender. Apples will release the water needed to make the syrup.

Optional: add raisins, walnuts or pecans

Gravy

Chicken or turkey gravy can be easily made without any milk. Use chicken broth instead if you do not already. To make the roux, use cornstarch instead of flour.

There are several ways to make chicken or turkey gravy.

Once the turkey is done retain the pan juices to make gravy, or you can use store bought chicken or turkey broth. I usually have homemade broth in the freezer but you can make some on the fly. Drippings or homemade is best. Save chicken bones throughout the year and use them to make broth, or, purchase a package of chicken wings or thighs and boil to make a wonderful broth. If you use thighs you can save the chicken and freeze it for casseroles.

Method One: you can make a roux by heating oil in a skillet, about 4 tablespoons and add 2 tablespoons cornstarch whisking until creamy and smooth. Immediately start adding broth one cup at a time. Add salt and pepper to taste.

Method Two: Heat the broth in a saucepan while reserving about ¼ cup of the broth in a small bowl or cup.
While the broth is coming to a boil add about six tablespoons cornstarch to the reserved bowl.
Whisk until smooth and creamy. Once the broth in the saucepan has come to a boil slowly add the cornstarch mixture while whisking the boiling broth briskly.
Turn the heat down to medium and continue to simmer until thickened. Add seasoning to taste.

If your family eats beef or pork, follow the same rules. I find chicken broth works well with ham or pot roast as well as turkey and chicken. If you prefer you can, of course, use beef or mushroom broth for your favorite beef dishes.

Green Beans

Green Bean Casserole

- 28oz can or equivalent cooked green beans
- Cream of Mushroom Soup

Ingredients:
¼ c. dairy free butter
1 cup diced fresh mushrooms
¼ c. diced yellow onion
2 diced garlic cloves
4 Tablespoons Arrowroot or cornstarch
½ c. Chicken broth
Melt butter in a skillet and add mushrooms and onion. Sauté until tender; about 3-4 minutes. Add garlic and stir. Sprinkle with Arrowroot. Stir to coat. Very quickly add broth, a little at a time, stirring as you add it. This should thicken quite quickly and be much like the consistency of Cream of Mushroom Soup you find in the can.
This can be stored in a glass jar and used within the week for Mushroom Soup (add a cup or so more chicken broth) or use in Green Bean Casserole as you would store bought Cream of Mushroom Soup.

- Gluten free French Fried Onion Crunchy topping: such as LiveGfree or you can make your own using fresh onions and cornstarch or rice flour.
- ½ cup chicken broth
- 1 teaspoon salt (or more to taste)

Preheat oven to 350.

Mix all ingredients except the french fried onions. Bake 40 minutes.
Add french fried onions to the top and bake an additional 5 minutes.

- One pound fresh green beans
- ¼ cup oil
- 1 teaspoon salt
- 1 teaspoon lemon pepper

Always blanch your green beans first!
Wait for the water to boil, drop your fresh green beans in, wait at least 5 minutes.
Remove immediately.
Toss green beans with oil, salt and pepper.
Spread onto a baking sheet.
Bake in a preheated 400 degree oven until golden brown.
Generally about 20 minutes. Be sure not to crowd the beans. Use two baking sheets if needed.

Use fresh or canned green beans.

Canned green beans: drain and rinse and instead cook in chicken broth with a bit of garlic, salt and pepper. Cook on the stove top, covered, allowing to simmer about 40 minutes. You can also cook with bacon fat.

Fresh green beans: wash and snip. Bring to a boil in water the first hour. Drain and then simmer in chicken broth, garlic, salt, pepper and bacon fat (optional) for another hour or so until nice and tender.

Greens

Collard Greens, turnip greens, swiss chard and spinach are all good choices.

- 1.5 pounds fresh collard greens, turnip greens or chard
- 6 slices crispy cooked bacon and save the bacon fat drippings
- One ham hock
- 1 cup diced onion
- 32 ounces chicken broth
- 4 cloves minced garlic
- 1/3 cup Apple cider Vinegar
- Salt and black pepper

Once the bacon is cooked remove it from the skillet and add the onions to the skillet.

Brown the onion until soft.

Crumble the crisp bacon.

Combine the bacon, onion, ham hock, garlic, broth, greens, vinegar and seasonings to a large stock pot.

Cover and cook on med/low about 2 hours stirring on occasion.

Spinach:

Using a saucepan, sauté a bit of diced onion, crispy bacon pieces in bacon fat or oil. Gently lay 2 pounds of fresh spinach on the top. Do not stir. Add about 3 tablespoons of apple cider vinegar over the leaves. Do not stir. Remove from heat and cover with a tight lid. Let sit at least 15 minutes. Stir before serving.

Legumes

The following legumes are soy free, gluten free, dairy free and nightshade free.

- Black Beans
- Black-eyed peas
- Chick Peas
- Green Peas
- Lima beans
- Navy Beans
- Northern Beans (white beans)
- Pintos

All good choices, canned (unseasoned except salt), dry, or frozen.

Stay away from canned baked beans due to the nightshades included in the ingredients.

Tip: When cooking dried or canned beans cook the beans in chicken broth for a deeper flavor. Tip two: be sure to salt the water or broth at the beginning of cooking your beans.

Parsnips

- 1 lb parsnips, washed and peeled
- 2 tablespoons cooking oil
- 1 teaspoons italian seasoning
- 1 teaspoon salt
- ½ teaspoon black pepper

Preheat the oven to 425.

Slice the parsnips lengthwise and toss with oil and the seasonings.
Spread out onto the baking sheet. Be sure to not overcrowd. Use two baking sheets if you need to.

Bake in the oven about 30 minutes. A knife should easily insert into the thickest part of the largest parsnip.

Spinach Salad

- Fresh baby spinach leaves
- ½ cup dried cranberries
- ¼ cup walnut pieces
- 1 small red onion chopped
- 2 tablespoons balsamic vinegar
- ½ teaspoon sugar
- 1/8 teaspoon salt
- 1/8 teaspoon pepper
- 3 tablespoons oil

In a hot dry skillet, sauté walnuts and cranberries for about 2 minutes. Remove from skillet and set aside.

Combine Balsamic Vinegar, sugar, salt, pepper and oil. Shake well.

Combine spinach, cranberries and walnuts, onion and toss with dressing. Serve immediately.

Sweet Potatoes

Baked Sweet Potatoes

I like to wrap my sweet potatoes individually in foil and then use the crock pot. You could also use an insta-pot. If you want to use the oven:

Wrap each potato individually in foil. Bake in a 425 oven until they smush. About an hour depending on the size.

Mashed Sweet Potatoes

Peel and cut one potato per person. Place in boiling water. Be sure you use a pot large enough that the potatoes have plenty of space and are covered with water.

Boil until very tender. About 30 minutes depending on how small you cut the potatoes. (before draining be sure to save the liquid in case you need it while whipping)

Drain well, add your favorite dairy free butter and mash and whip like you would any mashed potato. Be sure to salt! I find sweet potatoes get wonderfully fluffy if you use a traditional hand mixer to whip the potatoes. If you feel you need to add some liquid use the water you boiled the potatoes in or, you could use chicken broth.

- 1 large can yams or one pound baked, skinned sweet potatoes
- ½ can coconut milk, shaken well
- ½ cup dairy free butter or ghee
- 1 cup brown sugar
- 2 whole eggs
- 1 teaspoon salt
- ½ teaspoon nutmeg
- ½ teaspoon cinnamon
- 1 teaspoon vanilla extract
- ½ cup chopped pecans
- Marshmallows

Combine cooked or canned sweet potatoes, butter, sugar, milk, eggs, nutmeg, cinnamon and the vanilla. Beat on medium speed until nice and creamy.

Spray a casserole dish (no crust here unless you want to choose a gluten free crust).

Preheat oven to 350 degrees. Bake at 350 for about 40 minutes.
Top with pecans and marshmallows.
Return to oven until marshmallows have browned.

- 2 cups fresh, chopped yellow squash
- ½ cup sliced yellow onion
- 1 cup sliced mushrooms
- Cream of Mushroom Soup:
  Ingredients:
  ¼ c. dairy free butter
  1 cup diced fresh mushrooms
  2 diced garlic cloves
  4 Tablespoons Arrowroot or cornstarch
  ½ c. Chicken broth
  Melt butter in a skillet and add mushrooms and onion. Sauté until tender; about 3-4 minutes. Add garlic and stir. Sprinkle with Arrowroot. Stir to coat. Very quickly add broth, a little at a time, stirring as you add it. This should thicken quite quickly and be much like the consistency of Cream of Mushroom Soup you find in the can.
  This can be stored in a glass jar and used within the week for Mushroom Soup (add a cup or so more chicken broth) or use in Green Bean Casserole as you would store bought Cream of Mushroom Soup.
- ½ cup chicken broth
- 1 teaspoon salt (or more to taste)

Preheat oven to 350.

Chop squash and boil until tender. Drain and using a manual potato masher, mash up the squash. Don't use a hand mixer. You do not want it pureed. Just mashed a bit.
Sauté the onion and mushroom in a skillet before combining with the remaining ingredients.
Combine all ingredients.
Spread into a casserole dish.

Bake 45 minutes.

Tossed Salad

- 8 cups chopped romaine lettuce
- 2 medium red apples (gala), diced into bite size pieces
- 1/3 cup dried cranberries
- 1/3 cup chopped walnuts
- ¼ cup sliced green onions
- 2 tablespoons oil
- 2 tablespoons thawed cranberry juice concentrate
- 1 tablespoon white wine vinegar
- Salt and pepper

Toss the lettuce, apples, cranberries, onions, and walnuts in a large bowl.
In a jar combine oil, cranberry juice, vinegar, salt and pepper.
Toss with the salad and serve immediately.

DESSERTS

I would normally not encourage sweets, but this is for a holiday!

Menu ideas:

Cake and Pie

There are many gluten free cake mixes to choose from. If you are avoiding dairy soy, or nightshades please be sure to read the ingredients list before choosing. Many have potato starch (a nightshade), soybean oil and/or whey (a dairy). If you are unable to find a cake mix that is gluten free, dairy free, soy free and nightshade free stick with other desserts like pie, jello, fruit, and of course, *pie*!

If you are stuck on the store bought prepared icing here is a recipe:

Chocolate or Vanilla Icing

- ½ cup dairy free butter (softened)
- ½ teaspoon vanilla extract
- 2-3 cups powdered sugar
- 3-4 tablespoons canned coconut milk

Using a hand mixer cream the butter. Add the vanilla and the powdered sugar a little at a time. If the icing is thicker than you prefer add a little coconut milk. Add cocoa and more sugar to taste for chocolate icing. You can throw together a quick chocolate icing by combining cocoa, honey, dairy free butter and powdered sugar.

There are also pre-made gluten free crust that are pretty easy to find in most grocery stores. Check the freezer section or other section of the store where you normally find pre-made pie crust. There are several brands you can look for: Mi-del, Wholly and Kinnikinnick are three to look for. Use your favorite can of pie filling or your homemade recipe. Be sure to avoid soy, dairy and gluten. If you make your own pie fillings and use milk try substituting a can of coconut milk. If you traditionally use flour as a thickener, try using cornstarch or arrowroot instead.

Whipped cream can easily be made using full fat can of coconut milk. I have noticed some brands coming out with Dairy free whipped cream but please check the label as many of them include soy in the ingredients.

Chocolate Pie

- Gluten free pie shell
- ½ cup cocoa
- ¼ cup cornstarch
- 3 egg yolks
- 1.5 cups sugar
- 2 cans of coconut milk
- 1 teaspoon vanilla

In a saucepan, mix cocoa, cornstarch, beaten egg yolks, sugar and salt.
Then add the milk slowly while stirring over med/high heat.
Should thicken up.
Use a whisk to make creamy and smooth. Stir in the vanilla.
Continue to whisk until thickened to the consistency of pudding. About 15 minutes.

Pour into the pie shell(s). Refrigerate several hours before serving.

Filling:

- 1 cup sugar
- ¼ cup corn starch
- 1.5 cups cold water
- 3 eggs yolk
- 1 teaspoon lemon zest
- ¼ cup lemon juice
- 1 tablespoon dairy free butter
- Gluten free pie crust

Meringue

- 3 egg whites
- 1/3 cup sugar
- 1 teaspoon corn starch

Preheat oven to 350.

FILLING: Combine 1 cup sugar and the corn starch in a medium saucepan.
Add 1.5 cups cold water slowly, until smooth.
Remove from heat.
Stir in egg yolks slowly while whisking briskly.
Return to heat and bring to a boil over med heat.
Stir constantly and add lemon zest, lemon juice and the butter.
Pour into gluten free pie crust.

To make the meringue: beat the egg whites in a glass bowl with a hand mixer on high speed until foamy.
Mix in 1/3 cup sugar and 1 teaspoon corn starch.
Beat until stiff peaks form.

Spread this meringue over the pie filling.

Bake 15-20 minutes or until golden brown. Cool about half an hour before moving to the refrigerate to cool for about 3 hours before serving.

Preheat oven to 350

- 3 ounces dairy free butter
- 1 ¼ cup light brown sugar
- ¾ cup corn syrup
- 2 teaspoons vanilla
- ¼ teaspoon salt
- 3 large eggs
- 2 cups pecan halves
- Whipped cream (see recipe in this book)
- Gluten free pie crust

Melt butter in a saucepan over med heat. Add brown sugar, whisking until very smooth. Remove from heat and whisk in the corn syrup, vanilla and the salt.
In a small bowl beat the eggs and then add to the corn syrup mix.

Place the pecans in the pie shell and pour corn syrup mixture evenly over the pecans.

Bake about 45 minutes or per directions on your pre-made gluten free pie crust. If the directions only call for less than 30 minutes cook time, you can sauté the pecans in a dry skillet before adding to cut down on the time needed to cook through.

- 15 oz Canned pumpkin
- ½ cup Almond milk or coconut milk (carton)
- ½ cup Maple syrup
- 2 Eggs
- 1 teaspoon Cinnamon
- 1/8 teaspoon Nutmeg

Preheat oven to 400 degrees. Bake pie in a gluten free pie crust for 15 minutes. Then reduce your oven's temperature to 350 degrees and continue cooking your pie for another 45 minutes.

Dairy Free Whipped Cream

- One 15oz can full fat coconut milk
- 1 tablespoon sugar or more to taste
- 1 teaspoon vanilla or more to taste

The vanilla is essential when using coconut milk.

First you must chill the can of coconut milk in the refrigerator overnight. When you go to open the milk be sure NOT to shake the can. The fat has separated from the water and you want it to stay separated.

Open the can and drain off the liquid, or just scoop out the fat that has risen to the top and place the thick solid fat into a glass bowl.

Beat the fat until fluffy and light with soft peaks. Add the sugar and vanilla.

Jello

Marshmallows, not marshmallow cream

Green jello with fresh sliced red strawberries

Rice Krispy Treats

- 6 cups Gluten free Rice Krispies
- 10 oz bag of marshmallows (Avoid marshmallow cream and buy traditional marshmallows instead)
- 3 tablespoons dairy free butter or oil

In a large saucepan melt the butter or heat the oil.
Add the marshmallows and stir over low heat until completely melted.
Remove from heat.
Stir in the cereal until well coated.
Spread out on wax paper in your preferred container and press into the container. Work quickly!
Allow to dry and cool and then cut into single serving squares.

Additional Food List

Here is a list of gluten free, dairy free, soy free, nightshade free, NOT overly-processed foods that you can also choose from if they are not already listed above: While this is a good hearty list, it is by no means ALL of the foods that are gluten free, dairy free, soy free and nightshade free.

Beverage List

- Plain unflavored clean water

- Sparkling water; unflavored

- Almond Milk, Coconut Milk, Cashew Milk

- Coconut Water

- Coconut Milk

- Unsweetened, unflavored iced tea

- Herbal tea, green tea

- Soda, while not a healthy choice is gluten free, dairy free, soy free and nightshade free.

If you struggle with a grumbly stomach try switching to Distilled Water only. As in anytime you will consume the water used. Such as:

- Ice
- Soup where you will also consume the liquid (broth)
- Drinking water

No need when boiling foods and your intention is to discard the water

Vegetables

Fresh, frozen or canned. Just be sure the vegetable and water are the only ingredients. Some may also add citric acid for preservation. Also okay to eat. Avoid pre-seasoned vegetables.

- Acorn Squash
- Artichokes
- Arugula
- Asparagus
- Avocado
- Basil
- Beets and the Beet Greens
- Bibb Lettuce
- Black beans
- Black eyed peas
- Bok Choy
- Broccoli
- Brussel Sprouts
- Butter beans
- Butternut Squash (high carb so limit consumption)
- Cabbage
- Carrots
- Cauliflower
- Celery, celery leaves and celery root
- Chayote
- Chick peas
- Chives
- Cilantro
- Collard Greens
- Cucumbers
- Dandelion

- Dill
- Endive
- Fava beans
- Fennel
- Fiddlehead
- Frisee
- Garbanzo beans
- Garlic
- Ginger Root
- Green Beans
- Herbs
- Horseradish Root
- Iceberg Lettuce
- Jicama
- Kale
- Kidney beans
- Kohlrabi
- Leeks
- Lemon Grass
- Lentils
- Lettuce: all lettuce
- Lima beans
- Mung beans
- Mushrooms: All mushrooms [the exception to this are those of you with Candida or those who are vulnerable to getting yeast infections. You should also avoid aged cheese and nuts.]
- Mustard Greens
- Napa Cabbage
- Napoles
- Navy Beans
- Northern beans
- Okra
- Olives
- Onions
- Parsley
- Parsnips (high carb so limit consumption or avoid)
- Peas
- Pinto beans

- Plantains
- Pumpkin (higher carb food but less than a sweet potato or yam)
- Radicchio
- Radishes
- Rhubarb
- Romaine Lettuce
- Rutabaga
- Sage
- Scallions
- Snap Beans
- Snow Peas
- Spaghetti Squash
- Spinach
- Sugar snap peas
- Sunchokes (this is a higher carb food so limit consumption)
- Sweet Potato (high carb; limit consumption)
- Swiss Chard
- Turnips and Turnip Greens
- Watercress
- Wax beans
- Yellow Squash
- Yellow Wax Beans
- Zucchini

Refrigerated Foods

- Eggs

There are many dairy free products in the refrigerated department like butter, yogurt, etc. If you are also avoiding soy be sure to take a quick glance at the label before purchasing.

Frozen Foods

- Green Peas
- Peas and Carrots mix
- Onion, carrots and celery. Not to be mistaken with the bell pepper and onion. Avoid the bell pepper (a nightshade for at least the 45 Consecutive Day Intro)
- Broccoli
- Mushrooms*
- Cauliflower
- Chopped Greens: spinach, kale, etc
- Green beans
- Onions
- Okra (Not breaded. My favorite is whole okra for roasting in the oven or the sliced, unbreaded okra for soup)
- Berries, melon and peaches

You can also very easily freeze some produce foods.

- Garlic Bulbs/Cloves: just place in a freezer bag as is.
- Horseradish Root: just place in a freezer bag as is.
- Ginger Root: just place in a freezer bag as is.

- Turmeric Root: just place in a freezer bag as is.
- Onions: chop for future use and place in a freezer bag.
- Green Beans: blanch, cool freeze.
- Grapes: wash and de-stem. Place in a freezer bag.
- Berries: wash and place in a freezer bag.

Canned Foods and the Aisles

If a product you think should be included in this list is missing check the Vegetables, Frozen, Fruit and Beverage list.

- Almond Flour
- Amaranth flour
- Apple Cider Vinegar (Raw, Unfiltered "with the mother")
- Arrowroot (found near the cornstarch)
- Artichokes
- Anchovies
- Bakers Yeast and Active Dry Yeast
- Baking Soda
- Baking Powder
- Bamboo Shoots
- Black Olives
- Blackstrap Molasses (not in the 45 Day Consecutive Intro and after that sparingly!)
- Broth (or Stock): (Not bouillon)

    o Vegetable broth
    o Chicken Stock or Broth
    o Beef Broth or Stock
    o Bone Broth
    o Mushroom Broth

- Buckwheat flour
- Capers
- Chickpea flour
- Coco Powder: unsweetened cocoa powder to be used sparingly as usually when used we also add some type of sweetener.

- Coconut Aminos: often used to replace Soy Sauce
- Coconut Cream, Coconut Oil, Coconut Milk (canned), Coconut Water
- Coconut flour

- Cooking Oil: avoid soybean oil, canola oil, Vegetable oil which is soybean oil (look at the label). Nut, seed and fruit oils are fine such as:
  - Olive Oil
  - Sunflower Oil
  - Peanut Oil
  - Grapeseed Oil
  - Avocado Oil
  - Coconut Oil (there are two kinds: one does have the coconut taste and then a few brands that do not have the coconut flavor.
- Cooking Spray: not soybean oil or canola oil. If it says vegetable oil check the ingredient list.
- Corn Starch
- Fish Sauce (gluten free)
- Green Beans
- Hearts of Palm
- Honey (Raw, unfiltered is your best choice)
- Horseradish
- Kalamata Olives
- Lea & Perrins Worcestershire Sauce (this brand specific, not all Worcestershire sauce brands are gluten free)
- Nuts
- Nutritional Yeast Seasoning (great for a cheesy flavor alternative)
- Mushrooms
- Mustard
- Oats (choose gluten free to avoid cross contamination)
- Oat flour
- Olives (not the pimento)
- Oyster Sauce (gluten free)
- Pickles without spices in the ingredients list.
- Pumpkin
- Rice (if it bothers you it may be from cross contamination or you

may be sensitive to grains)
- Rice Flour
- Sauerkraut
- Sorghum flour
- Stock (or broth) Read the labels. Not all are treated the same! Better yet, make your own.
- Seafood: there are some canned/jarred seafood that is okay on occasion. Check your labels. Avoid those that include soybean oil, spices and sauces.
- Seasonings: Salt, pepper and anything not a byproduct of a nightshade.
- Seeds
- Sesame Oil
- Spring Rolls: if you can find one that uses tapioca flour and not potato starch or rice flour. If not use this product on rare occasion.
- Stevia: Avoid during your 45 Consecutive Day Intro. After that use sparingly.
- Sugar: brown, white, stevia
- Tahini
- Tapioca (check the label and avoid the ones including soy)
- Tapioca flour
- Vinegar: all vinegar with the exception of malt vinegar (a gluten). Any ingredient added to the vinegar must be on this grocery list.
- Wasabi
- Water Chestnuts

Meats and Seafood

In place of breakfast sausage and Italian sausage purchase ground pork in the pork section of the Meat Department. Add seasonings yourself.

- Breakfast Sausage: add sage, oregano, cumin, salt, pepper, garlic
- Italian Sausage: add Italian seasoning blend, garlic, salt and pepper.

Choose:

- Poultry: Whole chicken, hen, turkey. Ground turkey, ground chicken. Uncooked, unseasoned is what you are looking for. Bone in and skin on is what will give you a good stock or broth.
- Beef: Ground beef, steak, roast, ribs. Uncooked, unseasoned is what you are looking for. Bone in is what will give you a good stock or broth.
- Pork: Ground pork, pork chops, ribs. Unseasoned and uncooked is what you are looking for.
- Seafood: Raw, uncooked, unseasoned seafood that you cook and prepare at home is what you are looking for. If you are sensitive to sodium please read packages as some seafood's do have higher amounts of sodium.

Canned meats and seafood's because of their convenience and shelf life.

Look at the ingredient list on a can of tuna (they do vary but this is an example of one you would buy)

- Ingredients: tuna, water, vegetable broth, salt.

- All of those ingredients are included on this Grocery List.
- Not all canned tuna have those approved ingredients so please glance at the label before purchasing.
- Common ingredients in canned meats and seafood's you want to avoid are *spices, soybean oil, potato starch.

Fruit

Fresh, canned or frozen. Just be sure the fruit is the only ingredient other than possibly water, corn syrup and citric acid.

- Apples
- Apricots
- Blueberries
- Blackberries
- Cantaloupe
- Cherries
- Cranberries
- Grapes
- Honeydew
- Kiwi
- Lemons and Limes
- Melon
- Oranges and tangerines. Not grapefruit.
- Papaya
- Peaches
- Pears
- Pineapple
- Plums
- Raspberries
- Tangerines

- Tart Cherries (sweet cherries and tart cherries are not the same thing)
- Strawberries
- Watermelon

There are many gluten free products on the market today that you can try. Gluten free bread, pasta, and cereals. Just keep in mind that these are heavily processed foods and are still high carb foods. Always check the ingredients list if you are also avoiding soy and nightshades for soy products and byproducts as well as potato starch and the generic spices.

Nightshades can cause painful flares in those with chronic pain health issues. Arthritis is the most common. Stiffness, inflammation and autoimmune diseases that cause pain can be aggravated when we eat nightshades.

Legumes have also been known to trigger painful arthritis flares but they are gluten free, dairy free, soy free and nightshade free.

BONUS HOLIDAY BRUNCH MENU IDEAS

Eggs (scrambled, boiled, fried, or in a casserole), fruit, French toast, casseroles, bacon, sausage, cinnamon apples, cinnamon toast, sweet potato pie, hot cocoa, cinnamon spiced coffee, and all things wonderful. If you want to go big or go home, consider grilled steaks, fried eggs and a mimosa!

Baked Oatmeal

- 2 cups gluten free oats
- 2 large eggs
- 2/3 cups chopped pecans
- 2 teaspoons cinnamon
- 2 teaspoons vanilla
- 1 teaspoon baking powder
- ½ teaspoon salt
- ¼ teaspoon nutmeg
- 1 ¾ cup coconut milk
- 1/3 cup honey
- 3 tablespoons melted dairy free butter
- ¾ cup fresh or still frozen berries of your choice (blueberry or raspberries work best)
- 2 teaspoons sugar

Preheat oven to 375

Grease a 9 inch square baking pan.
Combine oats, nuts, cinnamon, baking powder, salt and the nutmeg.
In a separate bowl: combine the milk, honey, eggs, vanilla.
Spread half of your berries along the bottom of your baking dish.
Spread the dry oat mixture over the berries.
Drizzle the wet ingredients over the oats.
Shake the pan to help the ingredients to settle.
Pour the remaining berries evenly over the top.
Sprinkle with sugar.

Bake about 43 minutes. Allow this to rest about 10 minutes before serving. This does not necessarily slice into pieces but rather you would spoon it out to serve.

Banana Pancakes

- 2 large eggs
- 1 large banana
- ¼ teaspoon cinnamon
- ¼ teaspoon vanilla

Combine the eggs, banana, vanilla and cinnamon well. Brown just like you would any other pancake. Tip: these work best when you make smaller pancakes rather than large pancakes. As with other types of pancakes you will probably need to add dairy free butter or oil to the skillet prior to each new batch.

Blueberry French Toast Bake

- 6 eggs
- 3 cups coconut milk (in a carton from the dairy department, not a can) or cashew milk also works well.
- ¾ cup maple syrup
- 2 teaspoons cinnamon
- 1/8 teaspoon nutmeg
- ¼ teaspoon salt
- 4 slices of gluten free bread, cut into one inch squares
- 2 cups fresh or thawed frozen and drained blueberries
- 4 tablespoons white sugar

Preheat oven to 350

In a large bowl, whisk eggs, add milk, maple syrup, cinnamon, nutmeg and salt.

Add the bread pieces and coat well.

Stir in the blueberries and then pour the entire mixture into a greased baking dish.

Sprinkle some cinnamon and sugar on top. Bake about 40 minutes or until the filling is set and the top is golden brown. Serve with syrup.

Brown Sugared Bacon

- One package of thick sliced bacon
- 1/3 cup light brown sugar

Preheat oven to 325

Toss the bacon slices and the brown sugar in a bowl.
Arrange the bacon, in a single layer on a baking sheet.
If you want crispy bacon be sure to not overcrowd the baking sheet.
Leave a bit of space between each slice of bacon.
Use two or three baking sheets if necessary.
Sprinkle the remaining sugar on top of the bacon.
Bake about 20 minutes. Check, and bake longer if not done to your preference.

Egg Casserole

- 6 large eggs
- 6 slices of crispy cooked bacon or sausage (your choice)
- 3 tablespoons minced onion
- Salt and pepper

Preheat oven to 350

Whisk the eggs, onions, salt and pepper. Grease a casserole dish.
Pour the egg mixture into the casserole dish and bake about 15-20 minutes or until the eggs are just about set.
Add the crumbled bacon and continue to cook about 5 more minutes. If you have someone who can eat cheese and must have it, add some shredded cheese to a corner when you add the bacon or add it as soon as it comes out of the oven while it is still hot.

You could also make these in a muffin tin for individual servings.

French Toast

- 6 slices gluten free bread
- 6 eggs
- 1 teaspoon vanilla
- 1 teaspoon cinnamon
- ¼ teaspoon nutmeg
- 2 tablespoons sugar
- Dairy free butter or oil
- 1 can coconut milk, shaken
- Maple syrup or fruit topping

Whisk together the eggs, cinnamon, nutmeg, sugar, milk, and vanilla. Dip your bread into to briefly soak all sides of each piece.

Brown in a hot skillet with melted butter or hot oil.
Brown both sides and top with syrup, powdered sugar or a fruit topping.

Top with fresh sliced strawberries, bananas, or fried apples.

Fruit Salad

You could use any fruit but here is the suggested trio:

- Cubed cantaloupe (bite size pieces)
- Sliced or quartered strawberries
- Sliced kiwi

Dressing:

- 3 tablespoons honey
- 3 tablespoons fresh lime juice
- 3 tablespoons finely chopped fresh mint leaves (optional)

You can prepare the fruit ahead of time but wait until you are ready to serve to toss with the dressing.

Tip: mix the dressing before adding to the fruit.

Hot Cocoa

A luscious quick hot cocoa:

- One can coconut milk, shaken
- 4 tablespoons cocoa
- 4 tablespoons sugar or sweetener
- ½ teaspoon vanilla

Combine all ingredients. Heat through. You can even add marshmallows!

You can make this hot cocoa with any dairy free milk.

Smoked Salmon and Toast

- 6 large eggs
- 4 slices gluten free sandwich bread
- 1 tablespoon fresh lemon juice
- 4 ounces thinly sliced smoked salmon
- 2 tablespoons dairy free butter or oil
- Salt and pepper
- 3 tablespoons minced, fresh chives
- 1 ripe avocado, pitted, peeled and mashed (do this at time of serving)

Whisk together the chives and eggs.

Melt the butter or heat the oil in a skillet over med/ow heat.
Add the eggs and season with salt and pepper. Cook just as you would soft scrambled eggs.
Toast the bread and place on each plate.
Spread the mashed avocado onto each piece of toast.
Spritz with lemon juice, salt and pepper.
Spoon the eggs over the avocado.
Drape salmon slices over the eggs.
Garnish with any remaining chives, salt and pepper.

Spinach Salad with Warm Bacon Dressing

- One bag baby spinach leaves
- 8 pieces thick sliced bacon, fried crispy and then crumbled (reserve the bacon fat for the dressing)
- 2-3 large, boiled eggs, peeled and sliced
- 3 tablespoons red wine vinegar
- 1 teaspoon sugar
- 1 small red onion very thinly sliced (optional)

Transfer the bacon fat in a bowl.
Add the red wine vinegar, sugar, salt and pepper.
Whisk together well. Taste and adjust seasoning.
I will sometimes add a tablespoon of oil just to temper the vinegar a bit.

At time of serving, toss the spinach with the dressing and then add boiled egg slices and bacon to the top!

Sweet Potato Hash

- Peel and dice 2 large sweet potatoes
- Chop one large yellow onion
- 4 slices crispy cooked bacon and reserve the bacon fat in the skillet

After removing the bacon from the skillet, add the onion and sweet potatoes.

Add 2 tablespoons of water.

Cover and cook on med heat about 5 minutes.

Remove the lid and stir once.

After that, resist the urge to stir allowing the potatoes and onions to brown on one side.

Then, using a spatula, sort of flip them over to brown on the other side.

Once both sides have browned, then stir together to combine and serve.

****

Be sure to go to the Amazon Product page and leave a review! And be sure to check all of my other books:

www.amazon.com/author/paulachenderson

Made in the USA
Coppell, TX
09 December 2019

12626165R00056